Changes from solids to liquids to gases

A brief history

TODAY… 1851 Ice cream goes on sale in Baltimore, USA… 1842 It is discovered that salt will lower the freezing point of water. This leads to the development of frozen foods… 1761 Joseph Black, in England, discovers that ice soaks up heat as it melts although it doesn't change its temperature. Later he finds the same effect as water turns to steam… 1749 Knowledge of the cooling effect of evaporation, used in simple refrigerators in China for a long time, is brought back to Europe… 1712 Thomas Newcomen, in England, makes great developments in making the steam engine more efficient… 1698 In England, Thomas Savery builds the first pump powered by steam. It pulls water to the surface by condensing steam into water and creating a vacuum which sucks water from far below. The Steam Age begins… 1679 Denis Papin, in England, develops the pressure cooker (which uses steam under pressure to cook swiftly). The principles he discovers will also lay the foundations for the invention of the steam engine… 60AD Hero, of Greece, boils water to make steam and uses it to power a toy… 300BC Romans begin to use ice to cool the air. They also make the first ice lollies… 490BC Greek philosopher Leucippus invents the idea of the atom, the tiny particles from which everything is made, whether solid, liquid or gas. However, a proper theory of atoms will only start to be developed after 1803AD…

For more information visit www.science-at-school.com

Dr Brian Knapp

Word list

These are some science words that you should look out for as you go through the book. They are shown using CAPITAL letters.

BOIL
To change from a liquid to a gas very rapidly, producing bubbles as a result. Rapid evaporation of a liquid occurs both from the surface and inside. As a liquid changes to a gas it forms bubbles which rise and burst on the surface.

CONDENSATION
The change from gas to liquid. Water, for example, will condense onto the side of a cold glass, making it wet.

DEW
The change from gas (water vapour) to liquid water droplets that form overnight on plant leaves. This happens because the air cools during the night, and cold air can hold less water vapour than warm air. Some of the water vapour therefore condenses as dew.

EVAPORATION
The change from liquid to gas. Evaporation normally refers to relatively slow change. Boiling is a very fast form of evaporation.

FREEZE
To change from a liquid to a solid, often used to describe water. Every substance freezes at its own unique temperature. Freezing of water, for example, happens at 0°C. Freezing is another word for solidifying.
Heat has to be taken away from the liquid to make a liquid freeze.

FREEZING POINT
The temperature at which a liquid changes to a solid.

GAS
A form of a substance where all of the particles are free to move about. A gas will spread out to occupy all of a container it is kept in.

LIQUID
A form of a substance where the particles are free to slide over one another, but they remain attached. A liquid will always settle to the lowest part of any container it is kept in.

MELT
To change from a solid to a liquid. Heat is needed to make this happen.

MELTING POINT
The temperature at which a solid changes to a liquid.

MOISTURE
A word for water when it is a gas in the air.

MOLTEN
To become liquid – often used to describe liquid metal or rock (lava).

SOLID
A form of a substance where all of the particles are fixed together in a rigid way. As a result, a solid will not change shape to fill a container unless a force is applied.

STEAM
The name for water vapour produced as a result of water boiling.

VAPOUR
A word for water as a gas in the air. Vapour and water vapour are alternative words for the same thing.

WATER CYCLE
The continuous exchange of water between the sea, the air, clouds, rain, snow and rivers that happens all over the Earth.

Contents

Weblink: www.CurriculumVisions.com

How substances change

All pure substances can occur as solids, liquids or gases.

It is difficult to imagine a substance being **SOLID**, **LIQUID** and **GAS** all at the same time. But you only have to look at water to find an example (Picture 1).

▼ **(Picture 1)** Ice melts at 0°C. Here an ice bowl has been made in a freezer. As it melts in normal room temperatures, liquid water forms inside, which can then be poured out. At the same time, some of the water goes up into the air.

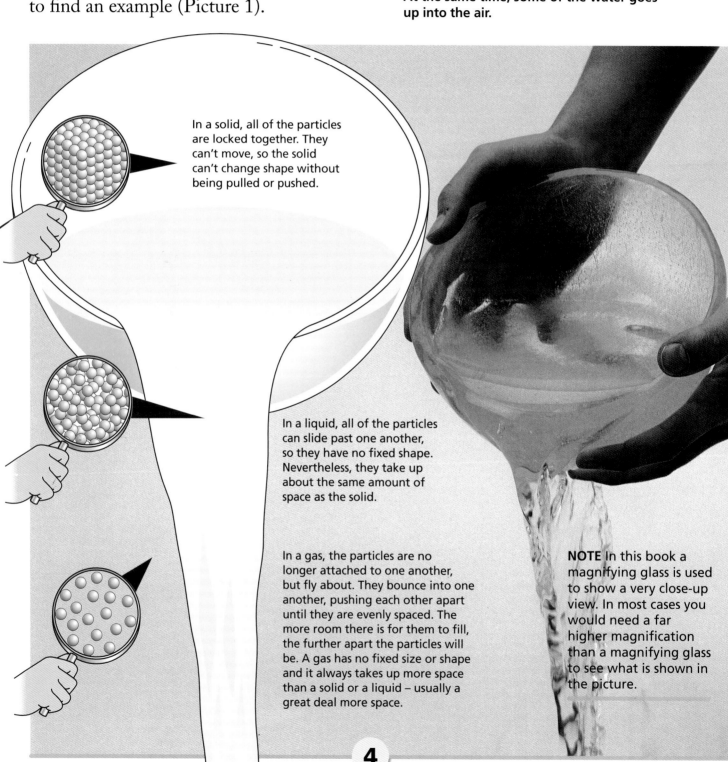

In a solid, all of the particles are locked together. They can't move, so the solid can't change shape without being pulled or pushed.

In a liquid, all of the particles can slide past one another, so they have no fixed shape. Nevertheless, they take up about the same amount of space as the solid.

In a gas, the particles are no longer attached to one another, but fly about. They bounce into one another, pushing each other apart until they are evenly spaced. The more room there is for them to fill, the further apart the particles will be. A gas has no fixed size or shape and it always takes up more space than a solid or a liquid – usually a great deal more space.

NOTE In this book a magnifying glass is used to show a very close-up view. In most cases you would need a far higher magnification than a magnifying glass to see what is shown in the picture.

Ice, water and gas bowl

You can make a bowl of ice quite easily. Simply partly fill a large freezer-safe bowl with water, and then put a slightly smaller bowl inside so that it floats. Put the combination into a freezer and let the water **FREEZE**, then remove the bowls.

As soon as it is taken from the freezer, the ice bowl begins to **MELT**, showing that ice and water are two forms of the same thing.

The water also loses some particles to the air. This is called **EVAPORATION** and it is how water **VAPOUR** is added to the air. In this way solid, liquid and gas forms of water can all occur at the same time.

These three forms of water occur naturally in the world around us. The oceans, rivers, lakes and clouds are filled with water, the ice caps and mountains are covered with snow ice (Picture 2), and the air is filled with vapour.

How does change happen?

When something melts, freezes or turns into a gas, the only change is in the way the particles of the substance are held together.

In a solid, the particles of water are all locked firmly together. In a liquid, the particles still touch, but they are no longer locked together and can slip over one another. That is why liquids flow. In a gas, the particles no longer touch, and are free to move wherever they want.

▲ (Picture 2) This mountain waterfall has been frozen into an icefall.

How to make changes happen

To get a solid to change to a liquid, heat has to be added. To get a liquid to become vapour, even more heat is needed.

The heat for these changes can come from the Sun, the warmth of the air or (in the case of **MOLTEN** rock called lava) from heat inside the Earth. People can also make changes happen, for example, by burning fuels to add heat, or using a refrigerator to take heat away.

Summary

- Solids, liquids and gases are different forms of the same substance.
- Solids are made of particles that are locked together.
- Liquids are made of particles that can slide past one another.
- Gases are made of particles that are free to move about.

Weblink: www.CurriculumVisions.com

Melting

When a solid changes to a liquid, it MELTS. Every solid has its own MELTING POINT.

A solid is made of particles locked in a fixed shape. A liquid contains the same particles but they are able to slide over one another.

Why solids melt

When a solid is heated, the particles get warm and begin to shake about. You can't see this because the particles are so tiny, but the jostling particles take up more space. As a result, as solids warm up, they swell, or expand. The more a solid is heated, the more it expands.

At a certain temperature, the amount of heat added allows the particles to shake loose from each other enough to slide about. That is when melting occurs (Picture 1).

The melting point

The temperature at which melting occurs is called the melting point. Ice (solid water) becomes liquid water at 0°C. The melting point of water is therefore 0°C.

Finding melting points

Many substances around us melt easily and this affects how we use them. If you put a bar of chocolate in a pan on a hot radiator for a few minutes it would almost certainly melt. So chocolate has a melting point that

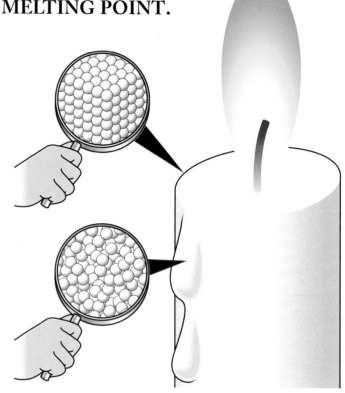

(Picture 1) This candle is melting, but only at the very high temperatures produced by a flame. The melting point of wax is far higher than the melting point of water.

(Picture 2) Wax only melts at the temperature of a flame.

Weblink: www.CurriculumVisions.com

is higher than room temperature (21°C) but lower than the temperature of the radiator (about 60°C). In fact, the melting point of chocolate is about 33°C.

If you put a wax candle in a pan on a hot radiator, nothing would happen, which tells us that the melting point of wax must be much higher than the temperature of the radiator (Picture 2). Butter is another substance that melts at a low temperature (Picture 3).

Using results like this you can make up a chart of melting points (Picture 4).

Summary
- **Solids melt and become liquids.**
- **Every solid has its own unique melting point.**

▶ **(Picture 3) The melting point of butter is less than hot water. This is why it melts easily when heated in a frying pan.**

▼ **(Picture 4) You can compare melting points of some common substances and make a chart of the results.**

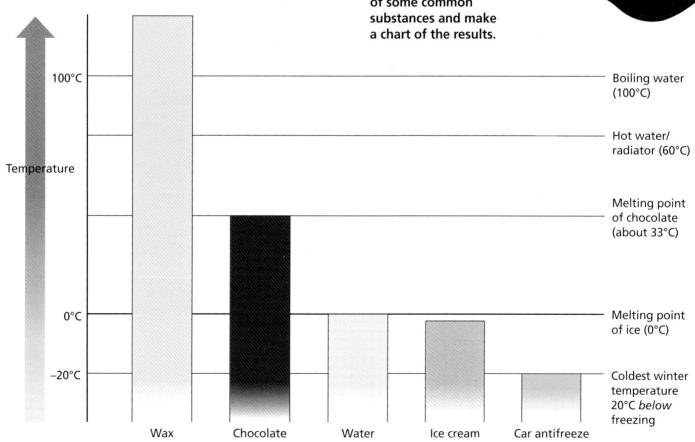

Temperature

Temperature	Reference
100°C	Boiling water (100°C)
	Hot water/ radiator (60°C)
	Melting point of chocolate (about 33°C)
0°C	Melting point of ice (0°C)
−20°C	Coldest winter temperature 20°C *below* freezing

Wax   Chocolate   Water   Ice cream   Car antifreeze

Weblink: www.CurriculumVisions.com

Why solids soften

When some solids get hot they gradually get softer as some substances in them melt but others do not.

◀ **(Picture 1)** Fat is solid when it is cold but is soft at room temperature.

▼ **(Picture 2)** As butter gets warmer, some of the links holding the particles together break, and the particles are free to move about. This is softening. When all the links break, the butter melts completely.

There are two kinds of materials: those that are made of just one substance, like water, and those that are made of a mixture of substances, such as chocolate, butter, glass and steel.

A pure substance, such as water, changes from a solid to a liquid suddenly. The temperature at which it does this is called the melting point. But mixtures of substances melt more gradually.

Solids get softer as they get hotter

Most substances are mixtures and so they melt over a range of temperatures. Thus, although chocolate melts at about 33°C, some of the substances in it will melt sooner. Chocolate then becomes soft.

If you put a tub of butter in a fridge so that it gets cold, and then scrape a knife across it, you will find that the butter is hard. If you then let the butter reach room temperature, you will find that it

Weblink: www.CurriculumVisions.com

has softened and can be easily spread (Pictures 1 and 2).

This happens because butter is a mixture of different substances. Some substances in the mixture start to melt before others. The warmer the butter gets, the more parts of the mixture melt, until finally it has all melted and become runny.

Melting mixtures

Steel is another example. It is a mixture of iron, carbon and other substances. Steel begins to soften when the temperature is about 1,000°C, but it only completely melts at about 1,536°C. The amount of softening matches changes in colour of the steel. Hot steel changes colour first to red, then orange, then, when it is almost **MOLTEN**, it becomes yellow. In a steelworks, the steel is heated until it is yellow hot and soft, and is then sent through rollers that squash it into sheets (Picture 3).

Summary
- Many materials get softer as they get hot.
- As substances in a material melt, the material becomes softer.

▽ (Picture 3) A yellow-hot bar of softened steel being rolled into a sheet.

Freezing

You can change the freezing point of pure substances by adding other substances to them.

When water changes from a liquid to a solid we say it **FREEZES**. Pure water freezes at 0°C.

When water freezes it turns into a solid – ice.

Mixing substances changes the freezing point

FREEZING POINTS of pure substances always stay the same. For example, pure water will always freeze at 0°C. But if we add substances to water to make a mixture, we can change its freezing point.

One easy way that we can change the temperature at which ice freezes is by

(Picture 2) Salt can be used to keep roads free of ice so they are safer to drive on.

adding salt (Picture 1). Once the salt has dissolved in the water, the mixture freezes at a much lower temperature than pure water. This is an important result. In winter, temperatures are often just below freezing, so roads become icy. But by spreading salt on the roads, so it combines with water, the freezing point of the mixture can be lowered to about 5 degrees below freezing. This makes it less likely that the roads will ice over (Picture 2).

Salt is just one substance that changes the freezing point of water. Other substances change it even more dramatically. Special liquids called antifreezes are added to the water in cars, so the water will stay liquid in all but the coldest weather.

(Picture 1) The freezing point of water can be lowered by adding salt or some other impurity. (In each case the liquid was stirred with the thermometer before the reading was made.)

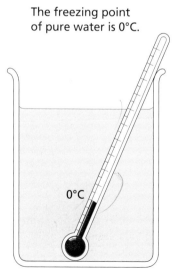

The freezing point of pure water is 0°C.

0°C

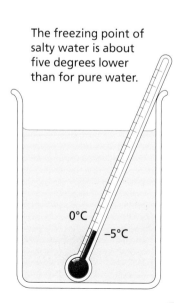

The freezing point of salty water is about five degrees lower than for pure water.

0°C

−5°C

▼ (Picture 3) Making ice cream.

Note: you must use a metal can, not a plastic or glass one for the ice cream because we want the cream to exchange its heat with the ice around it. Metal carries heat easily, whereas plastic and glass do not.

Step 1

Sugar

Whipping cream

Vanilla essence

Clean metal can with screw-on lid

Step 2

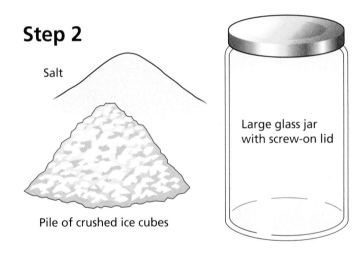

Salt

Large glass jar with screw-on lid

Pile of crushed ice cubes

Step 3

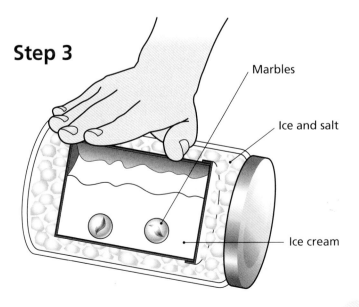

Marbles

Ice and salt

Ice cream

Using freezing points to make ice cream

We can make use of freezing points to make real ice cream at ordinary room temperature! Start with a cup of whipping cream, a quarter of a cup of sugar, and half a teaspoonful of vanilla essence (Picture 3). Put this in a clean *metal* can with a screw-on lid and stir well. Add a few (clean) marbles to the mixture to help do this. Screw on the lid. Now, crush about six cups of ice and mix in half a cup of salt. Put the sealed can in a big jar with a screw-on lid and pack the space in between the can and the jar with the crushed ice and salt. Screw on the lid. Now roll the jar on the floor. The marbles will move about as you shake or roll the jar and will help to mix the ingredients together. After about 10 minutes, stop rolling or shaking and open your ice cream.

By mixing ice and salt we have made a mixture that will begin to melt at a temperature well below 0°C. We use this to bring down the temperature of the cream below its freezing point and turn it into ice cream.

Once the cream has turned to a solid, take out the marbles, and enjoy eating the ice cream.

Summary

- Every substance has its own freezing point.
- We can lower the freezing point of a pure substance by mixing another substance with it.

Weblink: www.CurriculumVisions.com

Solidifying

When a liquid cools it turns into a solid. We call this solidifying.

▶ **(Picture 1) Moulding a jelly.**

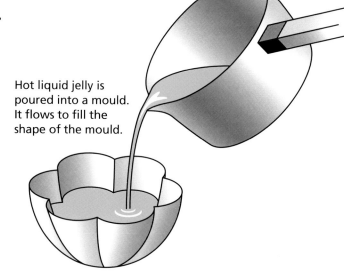

Hot liquid jelly is poured into a mould. It flows to fill the shape of the mould.

When a liquid cools, it loses heat. Usually (with water being the common exception), the liquid takes up less and less space as it cools. Finally, the particles start to pack together in a regular way. As soon as they do this, the liquid changes to a solid.

When water cools and changes from a liquid to a solid we call the process freezing. All other liquids 'freeze' and turn into solids as well, but we use the word 'solidify' instead.

Making use of melting and solidifying

When a solid changes into a liquid, it becomes runnier and can flow. When it cools again, it turns back into a solid. This can be a very useful property.

A jelly mould is a hollow container with a special shape, for example, the shape of an animal. Hot, liquid jelly is poured into the mould and then left to cool. Because it is a liquid, the hot jelly takes on the shape of the mould.

When the jelly has cooled down and turned into a solid, the mould can be turned upside down and the jelly gently shaken out. Because it is now a solid, the jelly will keep its shape (Picture 1).

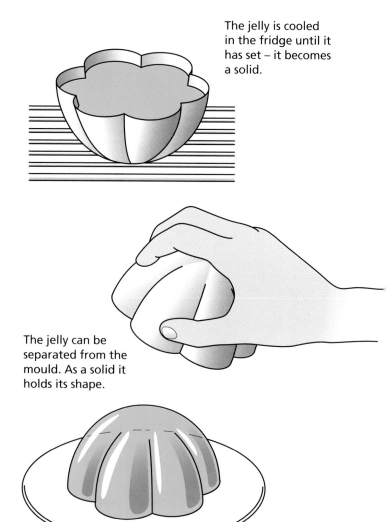

The jelly is cooled in the fridge until it has set – it becomes a solid.

The jelly can be separated from the mould. As a solid it holds its shape.

Weblink: www.CurriculumVisions.com

▼ (Picture 2) When making a cast a liquid is allowed to flow into a mould so it will form the shape of the mould when it solidifies. Even complicated shapes, such as this train, can be made in this way.

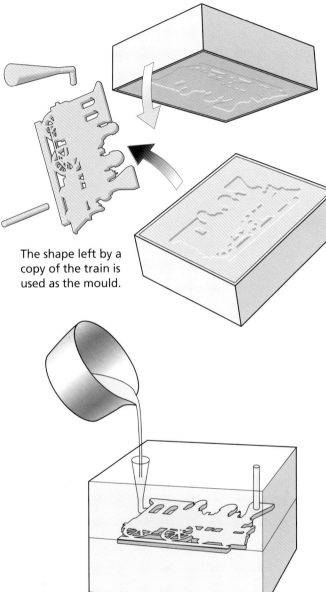

The shape left by a copy of the train is used as the mould.

Molten iron is poured into the mould. When it has cooled and solidified it is removed from the mould. The finished shape is called a casting. In this case it is cast iron.

The train is then painted and used as a door stop.

Casting

The casting process is used to shape many materials. Metals, such as bronze or cast iron, are heated until they are liquid and then poured into moulds to give them special shapes (Picture 2).

Glass bottles are made by placing a lump of molten glass in a mould, then blowing air into the glass. This makes the glass spread out and cover the inside of the mould.

Television screens are made by placing the molten glass in a mould and pressing it until it takes up the shape of the mould.

Plastic is also shaped by moulding. The liquid plastic is poured into a mould and allowed to cool and set to make a plate or bowl.

Summary

• When a liquid cools, it solidifies.
• Substances can be poured into complicated shapes when molten, then allowed to cool into solids for use.

Evaporation

When a liquid changes into a gas, it evaporates.

One of the most mysterious things in nature is the way a liquid will slowly disappear if left out in the open. For example, if spilled water is left open to the air in a warm room, within hours it will have vanished. We call this vanishing act **EVAPORATION** (Picture 1). The liquid has changed into an invisible **GAS**.

How evaporation works

To change a liquid to a gas, or **VAPOUR**, heat is needed (Picture 2). The source of the heat can be anything – sunshine, for example, or a radiator.

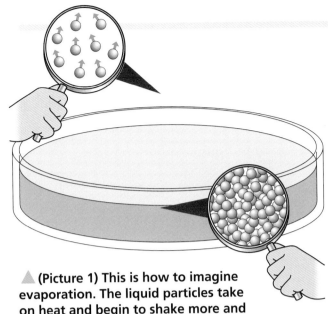

▲ **(Picture 1)** This is how to imagine evaporation. The liquid particles take on heat and begin to shake more and more violently until they shake loose and can drift into the air.

▼ **(Picture 2)** You can tell that heat is needed by noticing how much slower evaporation is in the winter, when the weather is cold. Streets may remain damp for weeks because there simply isn't enough heat in the air and the sunshine is too weak.

When there is lots of heat available, evaporation happens quickly. As the particles of liquid get warmer, they shake about more and more violently until, finally, the particles on the surface shake themselves loose. They then float off into the air as vapour. Because each particle of liquid water is colourless, and very tiny, water vapour is usually invisible.

There are many other sources of heat that cause evaporation. One important one is the air. Air stores heat (Picture 3). When the air shares its heat with the liquid, the liquid can start to evaporate.

◀ **(Picture 3)** If a thermometer is wrapped in a piece of wet cloth, the thermometer will show a fall in temperature. This is because heat is taken from the air as the water evaporates from the cloth.

14

One common example is in an airing cupboard. Here heat stored in the air is used to make water evaporate from the clothes.

Evaporation rates

Liquids evaporate when the particles they are made of get enough heat to shake free of the liquid. In some liquids, such as petrol, the particles are held together quite weakly and it is easy for the particles to shake themselves loose. That is why these substances evaporate very easily and quickly (Picture 4).

Water is an example of a liquid where the particles are held quite strongly. That is why water evaporates more slowly than petrol.

Some liquids evaporate even more slowly than water. Lubricating oil is one example.

Summary

- Evaporation happens when particles of liquid escape into the air.
- Evaporation needs a source of heat.
- Some liquids evaporate faster than others because the particles are bound together less strongly.

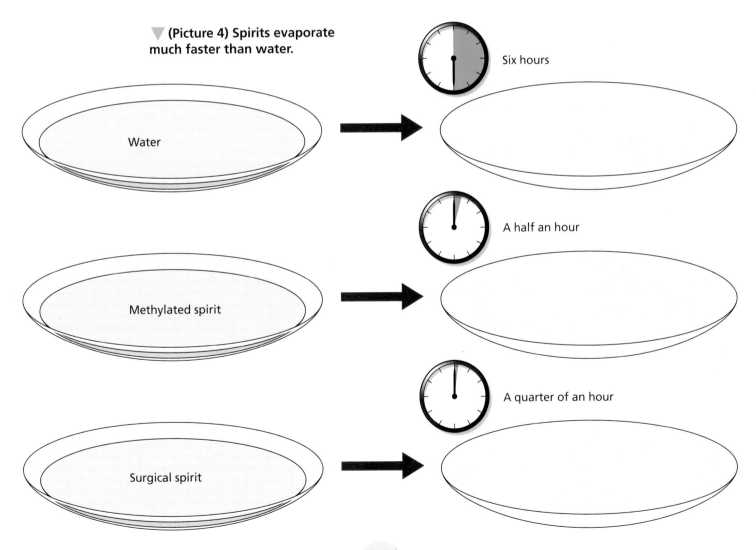

▼ (Picture 4) Spirits evaporate much faster than water.

Water — Six hours

Methylated spirit — A half an hour

Surgical spirit — A quarter of an hour

Weblink: www.CurriculumVisions.com

Boiling

When a liquid begins to bubble inside, the liquid is BOILING.

How do you know when water is boiling? You don't measure its temperature. You look at it and see if it is bubbling.

Why boiling gives bubbles

A boiling liquid is full of large, exploding bubbles. How do these bubbles form, and why do they grow?

Bubbling happens when a liquid has so much heat that particles start to shake themselves free of one another *inside* the liquid, as well as at the surface (Picture 1). The more this happens, the bigger the bubbles become. So, if you look at a gently boiling liquid you will see small bubbles, but a rapidly boiling liquid will be full of large bubbles.

In both cases, the bubbles contain vapour that has formed from the liquid. In boiling water, for example, the bubbles are full of water vapour. We call hot water vapour STEAM (Picture 2).

Why boiling takes time

There is a saying: "a watched pot never boils", meaning that you know the liquid is on the verge of boiling, but it seems to take for ever to boil. It takes time for a liquid to boil because the particles of liquid need to soak up a certain amount of heat before they can turn into a gas.

▲ (Picture 1) The bubbles that form inside a boiling liquid are full of gas.

▼ (Picture 2) Water changes between liquid, vapour and liquid again near the spout of a kettle. The liquid boils inside the kettle and vapour is produced. The vapour comes out of the kettle and is invisible (look closely near the spout), but the vapour is quickly cooled by the air and turns back into fine, liquid droplets we call steam.

Boiling safely

When a liquid boils, it is as hot as it can get. In the case of water this is 100°C. Splashes of boiling water and clouds of steam can be dangerous, so it is important to know how to boil water safely.

(Picture 3) Boiling gently (left) and vigorously (right and below).

Bubbles larger nearer the surface.

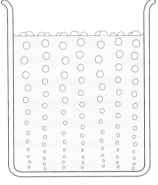

Rough surface   Smooth surface

The safest kind of boiling is when the bubbles are small (Picture 3).

Bubbles start on the bottom of the pan at places where the surface is rough. Water boiled in a pan with a rough surface, such as an aluminium pan, produces lots of small bubbles. These break out onto the surface with small splashes.

Boiling with a glass saucepan can lead to big splashes. The reason is that glass is smooth, so there are fewer places for bubbles to start, so the bubbles tend to be larger, rush faster to the surface and break more vigorously.

To prevent accidents with splashing hot water and steam, it makes sense to boil a nearly full pan gently, or use a deep pan with only a small amount of liquid, if you are going to boil it fiercely.

⚠️ **SAFETY** Never go near boiling water. Always get an adult to help.

⚠️ **SAFETY** It is always safest to put a lid on a saucepan to prevent splashes from the boiling liquid. The lid has been left off this saucepan for the demonstration only.

Summary
- Boiling happens when bubbles form inside a heated liquid.
- The bubbles are full of the vapour from the liquid. They are not full of air.
- The more fiercely a liquid is heated, the more vigorously it boils.

Condensation

When a gas cools, it turns back into a liquid. This is called CONDENSATION.

The air contains invisible water. We call this **MOISTURE** or water vapour. You cannot see, smell or taste water vapour – but it's there. However, you can sometimes sense that there is a lot of water in the air because it feels moist, or humid.

▼ **(Picture 1) Condensation forms on the outside of a glass of cold drink.**

Cold liquid

Glass

Water vapour in the air

Drop of condensation

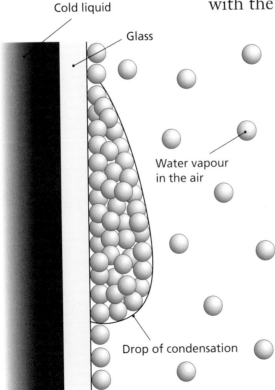

Condensation gives wet surfaces

When a gas blows against a cold surface some of the heat of the gas is transferred to the cold surface. The colder air cannot hold as much water vapour as when it was warm, so some vapour settles out on the cold surface and builds up into water droplets. This is condensation (Picture 1).

There are many examples of water vapour condensation on cold surfaces. A drink taken from a fridge will often quickly develop a wet surface. A single-glazed window will often be covered by condensation overnight, because the air inside the room was cooled by contact with the cold window.

Condensation happens outdoors, too. Early in the morning it is common to find a coating of moisture on the grass. This is called **DEW** (Picture 2).

Condensation in the air

The most common place for condensation to happen is high in the air. Here, it is responsible for clouds forming (Picture 3). The air contains countless particles of salt and dust that

Weblink: www.CurriculumVisions.com

are too small to see. When air becomes cold, these particles act as places for water vapour to condense onto.

As condensation occurs, we can start to see the tiny particles coated with water. We call them water droplets and they usually form clouds. Water droplets building up near the ground make it difficult to see long distances. A light build-up of these droplets is mist (when you cannot see beyond 1km). A heavy build-up of water droplets is fog (when you cannot see further than 100m).

▼ (Picture 2) Dew is one form of condensation. It occurs when leaves become very cold, usually at night.

Summary

- Condensation happens when a gas turns back into a liquid.
- Condensation occurs on cold surfaces, because they take the heat from the air.
- Condensation on the ground is called dew, while in the air it makes clouds.

(Picture 3) In cold air, droplets form on dust particles. They make the billions of water droplets that we see as cloud.

Water vapour in air

Water droplet

Dust particle

Weblink: www.CurriculumVisions.com

The water cycle: solid, liquid and gas

Moisture is all around us as invisible vapour. But when air gets cold, the vapour changes to water, or ice, in clouds and on the ground.

Water in the air occurs in three forms: gas (water vapour), liquid (cloud droplets and rain) and solid (ice crystals in the shape of snowflakes). By changing between gas, liquid and solid, water gives us rain, snow, moist air, oceans, rivers and lakes.

The never-ending change between the forms of water is called the **WATER CYCLE** (Picture 1).

How the water cycle works

Sunshine heats the ocean waters, giving the water enough energy to evaporate. Once turned into a gas, some of the water vapour is then carried high into the air by winds.

High in the air the heat begins to leave the water vapour, and it starts to condense onto particles of dust in the air, forming into tiny droplets. We see this as cloud.

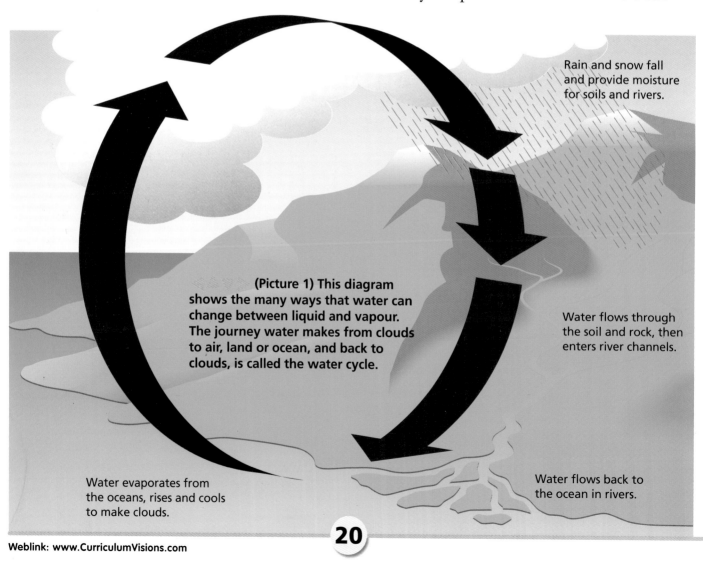

Rain and snow fall and provide moisture for soils and rivers.

(Picture 1) This diagram shows the many ways that water can change between liquid and vapour. The journey water makes from clouds to air, land or ocean, and back to clouds, is called the water cycle.

Water flows through the soil and rock, then enters river channels.

Water evaporates from the oceans, rises and cools to make clouds.

Water flows back to the ocean in rivers.

Weblink: www.CurriculumVisions.com

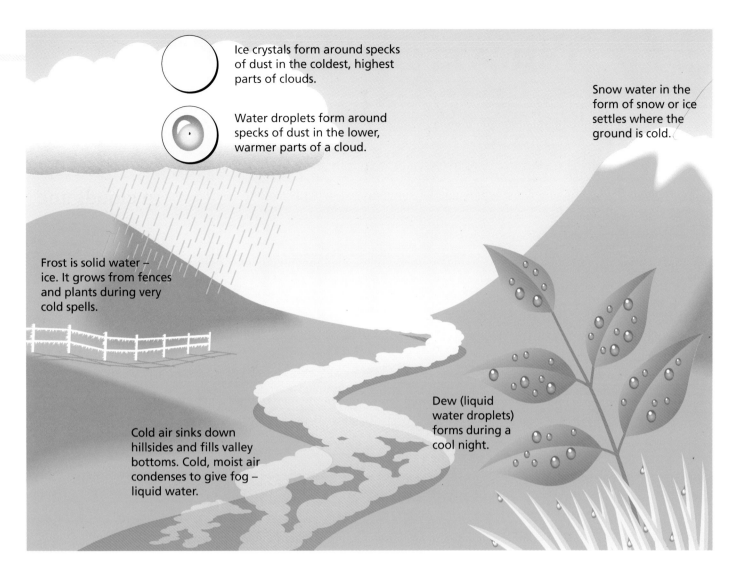

Ice crystals form around specks of dust in the coldest, highest parts of clouds.

Water droplets form around specks of dust in the lower, warmer parts of a cloud.

Snow water in the form of snow or ice settles where the ground is cold.

Frost is solid water – ice. It grows from fences and plants during very cold spells.

Cold air sinks down hillsides and fills valley bottoms. Cold, moist air condenses to give fog – liquid water.

Dew (liquid water droplets) forms during a cool night.

In some clouds, the air is so cold that water vapour turns directly into ice and snowflakes form.

From clouds to ground

Water droplets and snowflakes are carried about by the winds, often colliding and growing bigger. When they are big and heavy, they fall from the air as rain or snow.

Some air close to the ground also cools enough for water vapour to change to liquid water to give **DEW** (Picture 2).

Water droplets that reach the ground make surfaces like leaves, roofs and the ground wet. Once the ground is wet, any more rain that falls will seep into

▲ (Picture 2) This diagram shows the many ways that water can change between liquid and vapour. The journey water makes from clouds to air, to land or ocean, and back to clouds, is called the water cycle.

the soil, eventually reaching rivers and flowing back to the sea. At the end of each rainstorm, water evaporates off the wet surfaces and goes back into the air.

Plants take water from the soil through their roots, and lose it as vapour through their leaves, providing another route for water to get back into the air.

Summary
- **The water cycle uses changes between solid, liquid and gas to carry water around the world.**

What is green slime?

Some substances can behave like both liquids and solids without any change in temperature. This is what happens with green slime.

On the previous pages you will have seen how the same substance can have solid, liquid and gas forms. In all of these cases, the solid turned into a liquid, and then a gas, when it was heated. But science is full of surprises, and on this page you will find some substances that behave very strangely indeed, changing between solid and liquid simply when they are touched.

Green cornflour slime

Cornflour does not really mix with water. It seems to, but it stays as tiny pieces in the water. This is called a suspension. So it is not actually a liquid or a solid, but lots of tiny solid pieces spread out in a liquid.

If you make a very thick suspension of, say, five heaped teaspoons of cornflour in three tablespoons of water, and then mix in enough green food colouring to give a bright colour, you will have made a very strange substance, which you can call green slime (Picture 1).

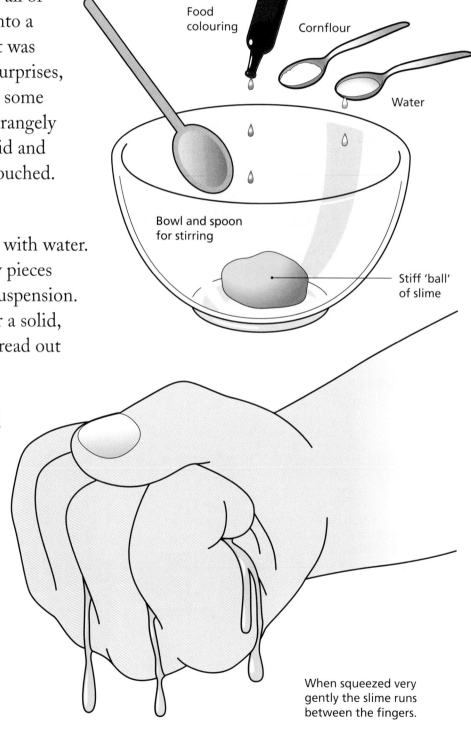

▼ **(Picture 1) Preparing the cornflour slime.**

Food colouring

Cornflour

Water

Bowl and spoon for stirring

Stiff 'ball' of slime

When squeezed very gently the slime runs between the fingers.

What happens?

A very thick suspension of some substances behaves like a liquid if it isn't touched. So it will very slowly creep down to the bottom of a mixing bowl just like a slimy liquid. If you put some in your hand and squeeze very slowly and gently, it will start to run between your fingers. But if you touch it with a jabbing motion, or squeeze it quickly, it will become 'shocked' and turn into a dry solid and can then be rolled up into a ball.

If you let the liquid flow off your fingertips, then waggle them, the

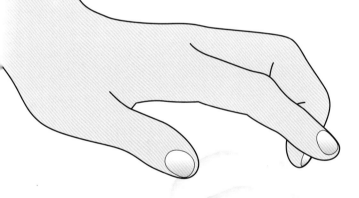

If the slime is 'shocked' by hitting it, throwing it against a surface, or grabbing it, then it goes hard and brittle and may crack on the surface.

NOTE When you have finished with the slime do not wash it down the sink as it may clog the drains. Dispose of it in a waste bin.

liquid will turn to a solid for a moment and you will have made a 'slime icicle'. (This can make a messy experiment even messier.)

Green glue slime

A different kind of slime can be made with white (PVA) glue and a substance called borax.

 NOTE Some people are allergic to borax, so wear rubber gloves during this experiment.

Start by stirring one heaped teaspoon of borax crystals into a small amount of water in a cup. Now put two heaped teaspoons of PVA glue in a bowl, add a teaspoon of the borax solution and some green food colouring and stir. You may need to add more borax, half a spoonful at a time, until the mixture becomes smooth and rubbery. Stir for a while longer, then make a ball from the mixture.

What happens?

You should be able to bounce the ball just as if the mixture were a solid. But if you put the ball onto your hand, it will slowly slime over the edges.

Summary

- Some mixtures are thick suspensions of solids in liquids.
- These mixtures will turn from liquids to solids if they are shocked.

Weblink: www.CurriculumVisions.com

Index

Science@School

Teacher's Guide
There is a Teacher's Guide to accompany this book, available only from the publisher.

There's much more on-line including videos
You will find multimedia resources covering this and ALL 37 QCA Key Stage 1 and 2 science units as well as history, geography, religion and spelling subjects in the Professional Zone at:

www.CurriculumVisions.com

A CVP Book
Copyright © 2002–7 Earthscape

First reprint 2005. Second reprint 2007.

Author
Brian Knapp, BSc, PhD

Educational Consultant
Peter Riley, BSc, C Biol, MI Biol, PGCE

Art Director
Duncan McCrae, BSc

Senior Designer
Adele Humphries, BA, PGCE

Editor
Lisa Magloff, MA

Illustrations
David Woodroffe

Designed and produced by
EARTHSCAPE

Printed in China by
WKT Co., Ltd

Volume 5D *Changing from solids to liquids to gases*
– Curriculum Visions Science@School
A CIP record for this book is available from the British Library.
Paperback ISBN 978 1 86214 160 5

Picture credits
All photographs are from the Earthscape Picture Library, except the following: (c=centre t=top b=bottom l=left r=right) Zefa 9.

This product is manufactured from sustainable managed forests. For every tree cut down at least one more is planted.